ASURI KESHAVACHARYA, A DEVOUT BRAHMANA OF SRIPERAMBUDUR,* PERFORMED A FIRE SACRIFICE AS HE DESIRED A SON.

IN DUE COURSE, HIS WIFE, KANTIMATI, GAVE BIRTH TO A SON. HER BROTHER, THE PIOUS SHAILA PURNA, CALLED ON THE COUPLE AND BLESSED THE CHILD.

YOUR SON WILL BE AS DEVOTED TO GOD AS LAKSHMANA WAS TO RAMA. CALL HIM RAMANUJA.

RAMANUJA GREW UP TO BE AN INTELLI-GENT BOY. HIS COUSIN, GOVINDA, WAS HIS CONSTANT COMPANION.

RAMANUJA IS VERY KEEN ON LEARNING.

* A VILLAGE NEAR MADRAS

1

WHEN RAMANUJA WAS SIXTEEN —

RAMANUJA MUST SEEK A WORTHY TEACHER TO CONTINUE HIS EDUCATION. PERHAPS WE SHOULD SEND HIM TO KANCHI.

FIRST, HE SHOULD GET MARRIED.

RAMANUJA WAS MARRIED TO A BEAUTIFUL GIRL.

A SHORT TIME AFTER THIS, RAMANUJA LOST HIS FATHER.

DO NOT GRIEVE, MOTHER!

RAMANUJA LEFT HIS ANCESTRAL VILLAGE AND SETTLED DOWN AT KANCHI WHICH WAS, IN THOSE DAYS, A GREAT CENTRE OF LEARNING. GOVINDA WENT WITH HIM. THEY BECAME THE PUPILS OF YADAVA PRAKASHA, A TEACHER OF RENOWN.

BUT RAMANUJA WAS NOT ALWAYS HAPPY WITH THE TEACHING OF HIS GURU—

PARDON ME, SIR. I THINK THE INTERPRETATION SHOULD BE....

HOW DARE YOU CORRECT ME! YOU MAY STAY AWAY IF YOU DON'T FIND MY TEACHING ACCEPTABLE!

YADAVA COULD NOT FORGET THE INCIDENT.

RAMANUJA IS YOUNG AND BRILLIANT AND HE IS CRITICAL OF OUR SYSTEM HE MAY LATER ESTABLIGH A RIVAL SYSTEM.

LATER HE CALLED HIS DISCIPLES TOGETHER.

WE MUST KILL RAMANUJA IN THE INTERESTS OF OUR COMMUNITY!

OH, NO!

BUT HOW, SIR?

WE WILL GO ON A PILIGRIMAGE. ON THE WAY....

I MUST WARN MY COUSIN.

AS PLANNED, YADAVA SET OUT ON A PILGRIMAGE WITH HIS DISCIPLES.

ON THE WAY, THEY SPENT THE NIGHT UNDER A TREE. BEFORE DAYBREAK—

RAMANUJA! YOU MUST LEAVE THIS PLACE AT ONCE!

WHY? WHAT'S THE MATTER, GOVINDA?

WHEN GOVINDA TOLD HIM ABOUT THE CONSPIRACY—

NO, GOVINDA, I AM NOT AFRAID TO DIE! I WON'T RUN AWAY!

YOU MUST—TO SAVE OUR TEACHER FROM THE SIN OF MURDER.

RAMANUJA FINALLY YIELDED TO GOVINDA'S PLEAS.

WHICH IS THE WAY BACK TO KANCHI? WHO CAN GUIDE ME EXCEPT· LORD NARAYANA?

THEN HE SAW A FOWLER AND HIS WIFE.

CHILD, WHERE ARE YOU GOING?

TO KANCHI. BUT I HAVE LOST MY WAY.

DON'T WORRY. WE WILL TAKE YOU THERE!

THEY WALKED SOUTHWARD TOGETHER. SOME TIME LATER—

SON, YOU MUST BE TIRED. LET US REST HERE FOR THE NIGHT.

THE FOWLER COLLECTED SOME WOOD AND KINDLED A FIRE. THEY WERE ABOUT TO LIE DOWN TO REST WHEN THE WOMAN TURNED TO HER HUSBAND.

I'M FEELING THIRSTY.

CAN'T YOU WAIT TILL THE MORNING? IT IS DIFFICULT TO FIND WATER IN THE DARK.

IN THE MORNING, THEY GOT UP AND RESUMED THEIR JOURNEY. AS THEY PASSED BY A TANK—

WAIT, MOTHER, I WILL BRING SOME WATER FOR YOU.

RAMANUJA PLUNGED INTO THE TANK AND REFRESHED HIMSELF.

THEN HE TOOK A HANDFUL OF WATER TO THE FOWLER'S WIFE.

MOTHER, HERE IS SOME WATER FOR YOU.

THE WOMAN DRANK THE WATER.

PLEASE BRING ME SOME MORE, SON.

WHEN HE HAD BROUGHT MORE WATER—

BUT WHERE HAVE THEY GONE ?

SUDDENLY—

THE TEMPLE TOWERS! I HAVE REACHED THE OUT-SKIRTS OF KANCHI!

RAMANUJA WENT STRAIGHT TO THE TEMPLE OF LORD VARADARAJA.*

LORD, IT WAS YOU IN THE GUISE OF A FOWLER! YOU CAME TO SHOW ME THE WAY! I DEDICATE MY LIFE TO YOU!

MEANWHILE —

YOU SAY YOU CAN'T FIND RAMANUJA? WHERE DID YOU SEE HIM LAST?

I SAW HIM WALKING TOWARDS THE FOREST, SIR.

PERHAPS HE'S BEEN KILLED BY A WILD ANIMAL!

ON HIS RETURN TO KANCHI, HOWEVER, YADAVA DISCOVERED THAT RAMANUJA WAS VERY MUCH ALIVE.

DOES HE SUSPECT ME? I'D BETTER SEND FOR HIM AND FIND OUT.

* ANOTHER NAME FOR LORD VISHNU

RAMANUJA ACCEPTED YADAVA'S INVITATION AND RESUMED HIS STUDIES CHEERFULLY.

HE HAS NO RESENTMENT AGAINST ME. HE MAKES ME FEEL ASHAMED OF MYSELF.

A FEW DAYS LATER, THE LOCAL CHIEFTAIN SENT A MESSENGER TO YADAVA.

HOLY ONE, MY MASTER'S DAUGHTER IS POSSESSED BY AN EVIL SPIRIT AND IS BEHAVING STRANGELY!

I WILL COME AT ONCE!

YADAVA WENT WITH HIS DISCIPLES. BUT HIS INCANTATIONS HAD NO EFFECT. IT WAS FINALLY RAMANUJA WHO EXORCISED THE EVIL SPIRIT.

O HOLY ONE, I AM INDEBTED TO YOU! PLEASE BLESS MY CHILD!

BURNING WITH SHAME AND JEALOUSY, YADAVA TURNED ON RAMANUJA AS SOON AS THEY WERE OUTSIDE.

YOU INSULTED ME! YOU SHOULD NOT HAVE EXORCISED THE SPIRIT WHEN I HAD FAILED!

8

I MEANT NO DISRESPECT TO YOU, SIR. HER SUFFERING MADE ME....

I WANT NO EXPLANATION! YOU WILL CEASE TO BE MY DISCIPLE FROM TODAY!

RAMANUJA LEFT WITH A HEAVY HEART AND RETURNED HOME.

MY EDUCATION IS INCOMPLETE. TO WHOM SHOULD I TURN FOR GUIDANCE?

IT SO HAPPENED THAT KANCHI PURNA, A DEVOTEE OF LORD VARADARAJA, AND A FRIEND OF THE FAMILY, CALLED THAT DAY—

YOU HAVE COME JUST WHEN I NEED YOU! I AM IN GREAT TROUBLE!

WHAT'S THE MATTER, RAMANUJA?

RAMANUJA TOLD HIM THE WHOLE STORY—

YADAVA IS A GOOD TEACHER. IT WILL BE DIFFICULT TO FIND ANOTHER—

YOU SHALL BE MY GURU! PLEASE ACCEPT ME AS YOUR PUPIL!

HOW CAN I BE THE GURU OF A BRAHMANA?

BEFORE GOD ALL ARE EQUAL! WHO AM I, THEN, TO MAKE A DISTINCTION BETWEEN BRAHMANA AND NON-BRAHMANA?

CHILD, YOU ARE ALREADY ON THE PATH OF TRUE LEARNING. SURRENDER YOURSELF TO LORD VARADA. HE WILL GUIDE YOU.

SO RAMANUJA WENT BACK TO KANCHI. THERE HE BEGAN TO SERVE THE LORD BY DAILY CARRYING WATER FROM THE LAKE TO THE TEMPLE.

ONE DAY, HE HEARD A DEVOTEE RECITING VERSES IN PRAISE OF THE LORD.

I WONDER WHO COMPOSED THOSE EXQUISITE VERSES!

RAMANUJA STOOD TRANSFIXED AS HE LISTENED TO THE VERSES. SUDDENLY HE REALISED THAT THE DEVOTEE WAS SPEAKING TO HIM.

I AM FROM SRIRANGAM. I AM LOOKING FOR A DEVOTEE CALLED RAMANUJA. WILL YOU TELL ME WHERE I CAN FIND HIM?

I AM RAMANUJA. CAN I BE OF ANY SERVICE TO YOU?

RAMANUJA WAS EAGER TO MEET YAMUNACHARYA WHOM THE SRIVAISHNAVAS* CONSIDERED AS THEIR GURU.

RAMANUJA AND MAHAPURNA WENT INSIDE TO PAY THEIR LAST RESPECTS TO THE RENOWNED SAINT OF SRIRANGAM.

* WORSHIPPERS OF LORD VISHNU

'IT SYMBOLISES THREE UNFULFILLED WISHES.

RAMANUJA CLOSED HIS EYES.

MASTER, I PROMISE...

TO PROPAGATE THE PATH OF DEVOTION TO GOD, WRITE A COMMENTARY ON THE BRAHMASUTRAS* AND PAY OFF THE DEBT TO PARASHARA.+

THE FINGERS HAVE STRAIGHTENED OUT!

RAMANUJA HAS DIVINE INSIGHT!

RAMANUJA RETURNED TO KANCHI—

THERE IS A LOT I HAVE STILL TO LEARN, BUT WHO WILL TEACH ME?

*A PHILOSOPHICAL WORK WHICH EXPLAINS THE ESSENCE OF THE UPANISHADS.
+A GREAT SAGE, FATHER OF VEDAVYASA

12

ONE DAY—

RAMANUJA, LOOK FOR MAHAPURNA AND STUDY UNDER HIM. THIS IS THE WILL OF LORD VARADARAJA.

I WILL DO AS YOU SAY, O KANCHI PURNA.

RAMANUJA LEFT FOR SRIRANGAM. ON THE WAY—

RAMANUJA!

SIR!

IT WAS MAHAPURNA.

RAMANUJA, THE SRIVAISHNAVAS OF SRIRANGAM HAVE CHOSEN YOU TO BE ACHARYA* AND IT WILL BE MY TASK TO EQUIP YOU FOR THAT HIGH OFFICE.

I WAS ON MY WAY TO YOU— TO LEARN AT YOUR FEET.

TOGETHER THEY PROCEEDED TO KANCHI. UNDER MAHAPURNA, RAMANUJA STUDIED THE SCRIPTURES SACRED TO THE SRIVAISHNAVAS.

WHEN THIS TASK WAS COMPLETED, MAHAPURNA RETURNED HOME. RAMANUJA WENT TO THE TEMPLE OF LORD VARADARAJA TO TAKE THE VOWS OF SANYASA.

LORD, I DEDICATE MY LIFE TO YOU!

*PRECEPTOR

RAMANUJA'S FAME SPREAD FAR. HE ATTRACTED MANY DISCIPLES, DASHARATHI AND KURESHA BEING THE IMPORTANT ONES. ONE DAY YADAVA PRAKASHA HIMSELF CAME TO HIM.

RAMANUJA, YOU ALONE CAN SHOW ME THE RIGHT PATH. ACCEPT ME AS YOUR DISCIPLE.

THE OTHER NOTABLE CONVERSION TO RAMANUJA'S TEACHING WAS YAJNAMURTI, A RENOWNED SCHOLAR OF THE TIME.

ONE DAY, THE SRIVAISHNAVAS OF SRIRANGAM CAME TO KANCHI TO CLAIM RAMANUJA FOR THEIR TEMPLE.

MASTER, WE ARE WAITING FOR YOU. PLEASE DO NOT DELAY ANY FURTHER. COME AND SETTLE DOWN AT SRIRANGAM.

BEFORE RAMANUJA COULD ANSWER, THE PEOPLE OF KANCHI STOOD UP.

NO! YOU CAN'T TAKE AWAY THE ACHARYA FROM US! WE NEED HIM HERE!

THE SRIVAISHNAVAS OF SRIRANGAM RETURNED DEJECTED.

IT IS UNFORTUNATE. WHERE WILL WE FIND ANOTHER TEACHER LIKE RAMANUJA?

I WILL BRING THE ACHARYA TO YOU!

THE DEVOTEE WHO HAD STEPPED FORWARD WAS RANGA PERUMAL, A GREAT MUSICIAN OF THE TIME.

RANGA PERUMAL WENT TO KANCHI. AT THE TEMPLE OF VARADARAJA, HE BEGAN TO SING DEVOTIONAL SONGS.

WHAT A MELODIOUS VOICE!

THIS IS A NEW EXPERIENCE!

WHEN HE HAD FINISHED, THE CHIEF PRIEST TURNED TO HIM.

SIR, NEVER BEFORE HAVE WE EXPERIENCED SUCH JOY. TELL US HOW WE CAN REWARD YOU. ASK FOR ANYTHING!

LET ME TAKE ACHARYA RAMANUJA WITH ME TO SRIRANGAM!

OH, NO!

NO!

BUT THE PEOPLE OF KANCHI HAD TO RESPECT THE PROMISE MADE.

RAMANUJA RECEIVED A ROUSING WELCOME AT SRIRANGAM.

LATER, WHEN MAHAPURNA CALLED ON HIM—

PEOPLE CALL ME ACHARYA. BUT I DO NOT YET KNOW THE WAY TO SALVATION.

GOSHTI PURNA OF TIRUKKOTTI MAY BE ABLE TO HELP YOU.

RAMANUJA WENT TO GOSHTI PURNA.

SIR, I SEEK YOUR GUIDANCE. WHAT IS THE WAY TO SALVATION?

GOSHTI PURNA DID NOT ANSWER.

RAMANUJA WENT TO HIM AGAIN AND AGAIN, TILL AT LAST—

I AM NOW CONVINCED OF YOUR DEVOTION. I WILL TELL YOU THE WAY TO SALVATION BUT YOU MUST PROMISE TO KEEP IT A SECRET.

I PROMISE!

GOSHTI PURNA WHISPERED IN HIS EAR—

OM NAMO NARAYANAYA!

THE NEXT MORNING, RAMANUJA CLIMBED TO THE TEMPLE TOP.

O MY BROTHERS! LISTEN! YOU WILL ACHIEVE SALVATION IF YOU REPEAT THE MANTRA, OM NAMO NARAYANAYA. BUT REMEMBER, WHILE UTTERING THESE WORDS, YOU MUST SURRENDER YOURSELF TO GOD.

OM NAMO NARAYANAYA!

ENRAGED GOSHTI PURNA SENT FOR RAMANUJA.

YOU WILL GO TO HELL FOR BREAKING YOUR PROMISE!

I DON'T MIND GOING TO HELL IF IT HELPS A HUNDRED OTHERS TO ACHIEVE SALVATION!

THE NEXT MOMENT, GOSHTI PURNA EMBRACED RAMANUJA.

A LITTLE LATER, THE FESTIVAL OF LORD RANGANATHA WAS BEING CELEBRATED AT SRIRANGAM. AMONG THE CROWD OF DEVOTEES WAS DHANURDASA, THE KING'S GUARD, ALONG WITH HIS WIFE.

THE SUN IS VERY HOT. LET ME HOLD THE UMBRELLA FOR YOU, MY DEAR.

THE OTHER DEVOTEES WERE SHOCKED BY DHANURDASA'S BEHAVIOUR.

SHAMELESS MAN!

SHOULD HE MAKE A PUBLIC EXHIBITION OF HIS LOVE FOR HIS WIFE?

WHEN ONE OF THE DISCIPLES DREW RAMANUJA'S ATTENTION TO DHANUR-DASA'S BEHAVIOUR.—

DON'T SCOFF AT HIM. A MAN WHO IS CAPABLE OF ABUNDANT LOVE, OBLIVIOUS OF HIS SURROUNDINGS, IS NOT EASILY TO BE FOUND. BUT THIS LOVE SHOULD BE DIRECTED TO THE RIGHT GOAL— GOD!

RAMANUJA SENT FOR DHANURDASA—

YOU LOVE YOUR WIFE DEEPLY. WHAT DO YOU SEE IN HER?

SHE HAS BEAUTIFUL EYES.

RAMANUJA TOOK HIM TO THE INNER SANCTUM OF THE TEMPLE.

LOOK ON THE LORD! HE IS THE MOST BEAUTIFUL ONE! HE IS EVERLASTING!

DHANURDASA STOOD MOTIONLESS, AS HE BEHELD THE LORD.

THE NEXT MOMENT —

MY LORD!

LATER —

YOU HAVE OPENED MY EYES. AS I BEHELD THE LORD I EXPERIENCED A NEW KIND OF JOY!

DHANURDASA AND HIS WIFE BECAME RAMANUJA'S FOLLOWERS TO THE DISMAY OF HIS OTHER DISCIPLES.

THE NEXT MORNING AS THEY ACCOMPANIED THEIR MASTER TO THE RIVER —

HOW CAN A MAN OF LOW CASTE BE ACCEPTED AS A DISCIPLE?

THIS IS A SACRILEGE!

RAMANUJA AND HIS DISCIPLES BATHED IN THE RIVER...

...AND SET OUT AGAIN FOR THE MATH.*

LOOK! THE MASTER IS WALKING WITH HIS ARM AROUND DHANURDASA!

OF WHAT USE IS A DIP IN THE HOLY KAVERI IF WE TOUCH A MAN OF LOW CASTE AFTER BATHING?

RAMANUJA WAS NOT UNAWARE OF THE GROWING RESENTMENT AMONG HIS DISCIPLES.

I MUST MAKE THEM UNDERSTAND.

ONE DAY, AFTER THEIR DIP IN THE RIVER, THE DISCIPLES RETURNED TO THE MATH TO CHANGE INTO DRY CLOTHES.

WHERE ARE OUR CLOTHES?

OUR CLOTHES HAVE BEEN STOLEN!

*A MONASTERY

THE DISCIPLES UTTERED A TORRENT OF ABUSE.

THE THIEF WILL GO TO HELL!

YES, HE IS DAMNED!

THEN RAMANUJA CALLED THEM.

SO YOU SUSPECT DHANURDASA! THEN GO TO HIS HOUSE TONIGHT WHILE I KEEP HIM ENGAGED IN A LONG DISCUSSION. STEAL HIS WIFE'S ORNAMENTS. YOU WILL THEN HAVE MORE THAN WHAT YOU LOST.

GOOD!

THAT'S HOW WE'LL TAKE OUR REVENGE ON HIM!

THAT NIGHT THE DISCIPLES WENT TO DHANURDASA'S HOUSE.

SH-H-H... BE VERY QUIET!

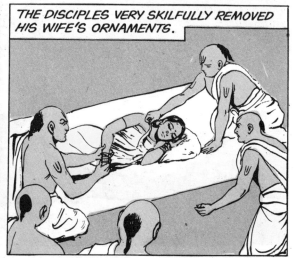

THE DISCIPLES VERY SKILFULLY REMOVED HIS WIFE'S ORNAMENTS.

SUDDENLY —

LOOK, SHE IS TURNING!

LET'S RUN AWAY!

WHEN THE DISCIPLES RETURNED —

DHANURDASA, YOU MAY GO HOME NOW. WE WILL RESUME OUR DISCUSSION TOMORROW.

DHANURDASA LEFT, AND THE DISCIPLES REPORTED THE SUCCESS OF THEIR MISSION.

GOOD! NOW, FOLLOW DHANURDASA HOME. LET ME KNOW WHAT HAPPENS THERE!

MY DEAR, YOUR NECKLACE AND ALL YOUR ORNAMENTS ON THE RIGHT ARE MISSING! HOW DID THAT HAPPEN?

SOME POOR BRAHMANAS CAME IN AND SLIPPED THEM OFF. TO HELP THEM TAKE THE ORNAMENTS ON MY LEFT ALSO, I TURNED BUT THEY FLED IN FEAR.

IF YOU HAD REMAINED STILL, THEY WOULD HAVE REMOVED ALL THE ORNAMENTS.

BUT YOU TURNED OVER BECAUSE YOU THOUGHT THE ORNAMENTS WERE YOURS AND YOU COULD GIVE THEM AWAY. MY DEAR, YOU MUST ROOT OUT THIS SENSE OF 'I'.

THE DISCIPLES REPORTED ALL THIS TO RAMANUJA.

JUST TO TEST YOU I HAD YOUR CLOTHES, MERE CLOTHES, HIDDEN. AND YOU LOST YOUR TEMPER. YET YOU HAVE SEEN HOW DHANURDASA AND HIS WIFE REACTED TO THE LOSS OF THEIR VALUABLE ORNAMENTS !

DHANURDASA IS A TRUE VAISHNAVA. HE HAS GIVEN UP ATTACHMENT.

RAMANUJA USED TO TREAT ALL, EVEN CHILDREN WITH RESPECT. ONCE, A GROUP OF URCHINS WERE PLAYING "THE TEMPLE GAME" ON THE STREET.

THE TEMPLE IS READY!

LET US WORSHIP THE LORD!

AFTER THE 'WORSHIP'—

NOW LET US DISTRIBUTE THE DEITY'S SWEET OFFERING.

THE CHILDREN GATHERED DUST AND OFFERED IT TO A PASSER-BY.

HERE'S SOME OF THE HOLY OFFERING FOR YOU!

THE MAN THREW IT AWAY, LAUGHING —

YOUR SWEET OFFERING IS OF NO USE TO ME!

WHEN RAMANUJA CAME THAT WAY —

THE TEMPLE OF THE LORD!

HE PROSTRATED HIMSELF BEFORE THE TEMPLE.

THE DISCIPLES WERE SHOCKED.

WHY, IT WAS BUT A PICTURE AND THEY WERE PLAYING A GAME.

IT MAY LOOK LIKE A GAME TO US. BUT THE CHILDREN SEE GOD IN THIS TEMPLE AND, THEREFORE, *HE* IS HERE!

LATER RAMANUJA WENT TO TIRUPATI ON A PILGRIMAGE.

LORD VENKATESHA!

WHILE HE WAS WALKING HOME FROM THE TEMPLE —

WHAT'S THIS? A MAN PUTTING HIS HAND INTO THE MOUTH OF A SNAKE?

IT'S YOU, GOVINDA!

JUST A MOMENT! I AM REMOVING A THORN WHICH HAS GOT STUCK IN THE TONGUE OF THIS POOR CREATURE.

WHEN GOVINDA FINISHED HIS WORK AND GOT UP, RAMANUJA EMBRACED HIM.

YOU ARE A TRUE VAISHNAVA— COMPASSIONATE AND HELPFUL.

ACHARYA! PLEASE ACCEPT ME AS YOUR DISCIPLE!

THEY RETURNED TO SRIRANGAM —

I HAVE A WORTHY DISCIPLE IN GOVINDA. NOW IS THE TIME TO FULFIL THE PLEDGE TO YAMUNACHARYA. I MUST WRITE THE COMMENTARY ON THE BRAHMASUTRAS.

RAMANUJA LEFT WITH HIS DISCIPLES FOR FAR-AWAY KASHMIR, TO PROCURE AND STUDY AN OLD COMMENTARY ON THE BRAHMASUTRAS BY THE PHILOSOPHER, BODHAYANA.

ON REACHING KASHMIR, HE CALLED ON THE SCHOLARS THERE, AND TOLD THEM WHAT HE WANTED. BUT —

NO, WE CANNOT PART WITH THE PRECIOUS WORK OF REVERED BODHAYANA.

THEN RAMANUJA SOUGHT THE HELP OF THE KING OF KASHMIR.

KNOWLEDGE BELONGS TO ALL WHO SEEK IT. PLEASE MAKE BODHAYANA'S WORK AVAILABLE TO US.

THE KING WAS VERY IMPRESSED BY THE FORCE OF RAMANUJA'S ARGUMENTS AND BY HIS PERSONALITY.

THE ACHARYA IS RIGHT. GIVE HIM THE WORK OF BODHA-YANA. HE CAN TAKE IT TO SRIRANGAM.

WE BOW TO YOUR WISHES.

KURESHA, ONE OF RAMANUJA'S DISCIPLES, STEPPED FORWARD AND RECEIVED BODHA-YANA'S WORK.

YOU WON'T KEEP THIS FOR LONG.

THE NEXT DAY THEY BEGAN THEIR JOURNEY BACK TO SRIRANGAM. SUDDENLY—

SURRENDER THE WORK, IF YOU VALUE YOUR LIFE!

THUS THE PRECIOUS WORK WAS TAKEN AWAY BY FORCE. BUT—

ACHARYA, DON'T WORRY. I SPENT THE WHOLE NIGHT READING IT. I HAVE MEMORISED EVERY WORD.

HOW GLAD I AM TO HEAR YOU SAY THIS, KURESHA!

AT SRIRANGAM, KURESHA MADE A COPY OF BODHAYANA'S COMMENTARY FROM MEMORY. RAMANUJA STUDIED IT AND WROTE 'SRIBHASHYA', A COMMENTARY ON THE BRAHMASUTRAS.

RAMANUJA ALSO WROTE "VEDARTHA SANGRAHA," A WORK ON THE UPANISHADS, THE 'GITA BHASHYA,' A COMMENTARY ON THE GITA, AND OTHER WORKS.

WHEN RAMANUJA WAS SEVENTY-NINE YEARS OLD, HE HAD TO LEAVE SRIRANGAM AS THE KING HAD BEGUN TO PERSECUTE THE SRIVAISHNAVAS.

HOWEVER, HE RECEIVED A WARM WELCOME IN THE HOYSALA KINGDOM IN KARNATAKA. KING BITTIDEVA HIMSELF RECEIVED HIM.

MASTER, MAKE KARNATAKA YOUR HOME AND BLESS US.

BITTIDEVA BECAME RAMANUJA'S DISCIPLE AND ASSUMED THE NAME 'VISHNU VARDHANA'.

RAMANUJA TOURED KARNATAKA AND SPREAD THE SRIVAISHNAVA PHILOSOPHY. ONCE WHILE PASSING THROUGH A FOREST NEAR YADUGIRI*—

HM, THE FRAGRANCE OF THE TULSI PLANT!

HE FOLLOWED THE SCENT—

THE FRAGRANCE EMANATES FROM THIS ANT-HILL. DIG IT UP!

LAYERS OF EARTH WERE DUG AWAY AND...

...RAMANUJA BENT DOWN AND RETRIEVED AN IDOL OF NARAYANA.

MY LORD!

RAMANUJA HAD A TEMPLE BUILT THERE AND CONSECRATED THE IDOL. LATER, SOME OF THE ELDERS OF YADU-GIRI CAME TO HIM.

YEARS AGO, WHEN INVADERS RANSACKED YADUGIRI, WE MANAGED TO HIDE TWO IDOLS. YOU HAVE FOUND ONE. THE OTHER IDOL OF RAMAPRIYA IS IN DELHI, IN THE HOUSE OF A MUSLIM NOBLEMAN.

DON'T WORRY, I WILL BRING IT BACK!

* THE MODERN MELKOT, NEAR MYSORE

RAMANUJA CALLED ON THE NOBLEMAN AND OBTAINED THE IDOL. HE SET OUT ON HIS RETURN JOURNEY. WHEN HE HAD ALMOST REACHED YADUGIRI, A GROUP OF RAIDERS OVERTOOK HIM.

THAT'S OUR MAN!

YES, HE HAS THE IDOL!

THEY SURROUNDED HIM.

GIVE US BACK THE IDOL!

BUT THE NOBLEMAN HIMSELF GAVE IT TO ME!

HE HAD SECOND THOUGHTS AFTER YOU LEFT. HIS DAUGHTER WANTS IT BACK.

JUST THEN, A GROUP OF VILLAGERS HAPPENED TO PASS BY—

LOOK! THE HOLY ONE IS SURROUNDED!

QUICK! TO THE RESCUE!

THEY FELL UPON THE RAIDERS FROM DELHI AND DROVE THEM AWAY.

LORD NARAYANA IS PLEASED WITH YOU. COME TO THE TEMPLE AND RECEIVE HIS BLESSINGS!

WE CAN'T! WE ARE UNTOUCHABLES!

YOU ARE CHILDREN OF GOD! BELIEVE ME, THE ALL-PERVADING GOD RESIDES IN YOU, TOO!

RAMANUJA THREW OPEN THE TEMPLE OF TIRU NARAYANA AT YADUGIRI TO ALL CASTES.

LATER, RAMANUJA RETURNED TO SRIRANGAM, WHERE HE SPENT THE REST OF HIS LIFE.